Aug. 3, 2003

Bestest Friend,

Happy Birthday. Thank
you for being there
I need you. Bonn

My Dear Friend

HOLLY POND HILL®
BY SUSAN WHEELER

HARVEST HOUSE PUBLISHERS
Eugene, Oregon

My Dear Friend

Text copyright © 2001 by Harvest House Publishers
Eugene, Oregon 97402

ISBN 0-7369-0506-5

Design and production by Garborg Design Works, Minneapolis, Minnesota

Harvest House Publishers has made every effort to trace the ownership of all poems and quotes. In the event of a question arising from the use of a poem or quote, we regret any error made and will be pleased to make the necessary correction in future editions of this book.

Scripture quotations are taken from the Holy Bible, New International Version®, Copyright © 1973, 1978, 1984 by the International Bible Society. Used by permission of Zondervan Publishing House.

Printed in Hong Kong.

01 02 03 04 05 06 07 08 09 10 / NG / 10 9 8 7 6 5 4 3 2 1

How rare and wonderful
is that flash of a moment
when we realize we have
discovered a friend.

WILLIAM E. ROTHSCHILD

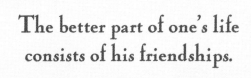

The better part of one's life
consists of his friendships.

ABRAHAM LINCOLN

Good friends are good for your health.

IRWIN SARASON

Life is to be fortified
by many friendships.
To love and to be loved
is the greatest happiness
of existence.

SYDNEY SMITH

The road to

a friend's

house is

never long.

**DANISH
PROVERB**

Breathless, we flung us on the windy hill,
Laughed in the sun, and kissed the lovely grass.

RUPERT BROOKE

Oh the comfort, the
inexpressible comfort
of feeling safe with a
person; having neither
to weigh thoughts nor
measure words...

MARIAN EVANS

7

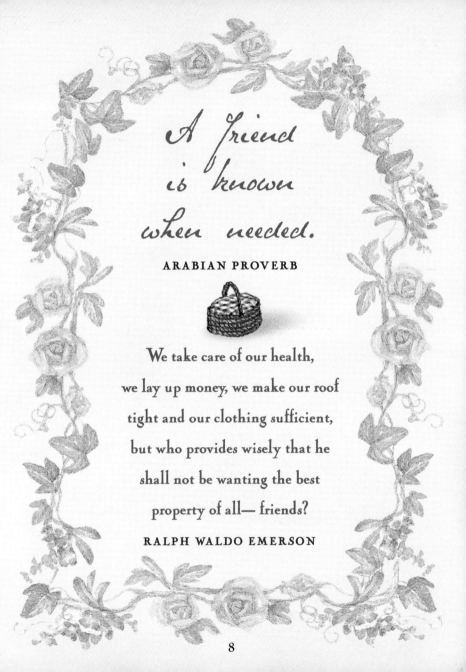

*A friend
is known
when needed.*

ARABIAN PROVERB

We take care of our health,
we lay up money, we make our roof
tight and our clothing sufficient,
but who provides wisely that he
shall not be wanting the best
property of all— friends?

RALPH WALDO EMERSON

Who finds a
faithful friend,
finds a treasure.

**JEWISH
PROVERB**

We need old friends to help us grow old and new friends to help us stay young.

LETTY COTTIN POGREBIN

A Friend may well be reckoned the masterpiece of Nature.

RALPH WALDO EMERSON

The only good teachers for you are those friends who love you, who think you are interesting, or very important, or wonderfully funny.

BRENDA UELAND

I am speaking now of the highest duty we owe our friends, the noblest, the most sacred — that of keeping their own nobleness, goodness, pure and incorrupt.

HARRIET BEECHER STOWE

Friends and good
manners will carry
you where money
won't go.

MARGARET WALKER

13

1 Corinthians 15:56

Susan Wheeler

The man who treasures his friends is
usually solid gold himself.

MARJORIE HOLMES

Treat your friends as
you do your pictures,
and place them
in their best light.

JENNIE JEROME
CHURCHILL

It is wise to apply the oil of refined politeness
to the mechanism of friendship.

COLETTE

Best friend, my well-spring
in the wilderness!
GEORGE ELIOT

I had three chairs in
my house; one for
solitude, two for friendship,
three for society.

HENRY DAVID
THOREAU

e have been friends together
In sunshine and in shade.

CAROLINE SHERIDAN NORTON

17

Friends are the thermometer by which we may judge the temperature of our fortunes.

LADY MARGUERITE
BLESSINGTON

Susan Wheeler

A home-made
friend wears
longer than
one you buy
in the market.

**AUSTIN
O'MALLEY**

My only sketch, profile,
of Heaven is a large
blue sky, and larger
than the biggest I have
seen in June—and in
it are my friends—
every one of them.

EMILY DICKINSON

*A friend is a
person with whom
I may be sincere.
Before him I
may think aloud.*

**RALPH WALDO
EMERSON**

Friendship redoubleth
joys, and cutteth
griefs in half.

FRANCIS BACON

The worst solitude is to be
destitute of sincere friendship.

FRANCIS BACON

You don't just
luck into things as
much as you'd like to
think you do. You
build step by step,
whether it's friendships
or opportunities.

BARBARA BUSH

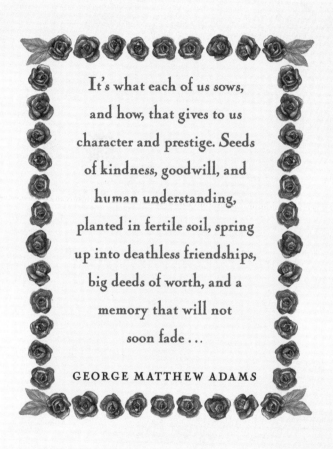

It's what each of us sows,
and how, that gives to us
character and prestige. Seeds
of kindness, goodwill, and
human understanding,
planted in fertile soil, spring
up into deathless friendships,
big deeds of worth, and a
memory that will not
soon fade ...

GEORGE MATTHEW ADAMS

Could we see when and where we would meet again, we would be more tender when we bid our friends goodbye.

OUIDA

Friendship without self-interest is one of the rare and beautiful things of life.

JAMES F. BYRNES

If I were to name the three most precious resources of life, I should say books, friends, and nature...

JOHN BURROUGHS

If you want an accounting of your worth, count your friends.

MERRY BROWNE

No love, no friendship can cross
the path of our destiny without
leaving some mark on it forever.

FRANCOIS MAURIAC

Promises may get friends,
but it is performance that
must nurse and keep them.

OWEN FELTHAM

Susan Wheeler

True friendship
brings sunshine
to the shade, and
shade to the
sunshine.

THOMAS BURKE

The ornament of a house is the friends who frequent it.

RALPH WALDO EMERSON

The best friend
is the man who
in wishing me
well wishes it
for my sake.

ARISTOTLE

> **A faithful friend is a strong defense; and he that hath found him hath found a treasure.**
>
> LOUISA MAY ALCOTT

If I don't have friends, then I ain't nothing.

BILLIE HOLIDAY

Two are better than one, because they have a good return for their work: If one falls down, his friend can help him up.

THE BOOK OF ECCLESIASTES

Nobody sees a
flower really; it
is so small.
We haven't time,
and to see takes
time—like to
have a friend
takes time.

GEORGIA O'KEEFFE

My friends
are my estate.

EMILY
DICKINSON

37

Wishing to be friends is quick work,
but friendship is a slow-ripening fruit.

ARISTOTLE

*A man cannot
be said to succeed
in this life who
does not satisfy
one friend.*

HENRY DAVID THOREAU

A single rose
can be my
garden...
a single friend,
my world.
LEO BUSCAGLIA

A slender acquaintance with the world
must convince every man that actions,
not words, are the true criterion of the
attachment of friends.

GEORGE WASHINGTON

Cherish your human
connections: your relationships
with friends and family.

BARBARA BUSH

Friends are as
companions on
a journey, who
ought to aid each
other to persevere
in the road to a
happier life.

PYTHAGORAS

Friendship is the only thing in the world concerning the usefulness of which all mankind are agreed.

MARCUS TULLIUS CICERO

He who sows courtesy reaps friendship, and he who plants kindness gathers love.

SAINT BASIL

Our friends interpret the world and ourselves to us, if we take them tenderly and truly.

AMOS BRONSON ALCOTT

Perhaps the most delightful friendships are

those in which there is much agreement, much

disputation, and yet more personal liking.

GEORGE ELIOT

The glory of friendship is not in the outstretched
hand, nor the kindly smile, nor the joy of
companionship; it is in the spiritual inspiration
that comes to one when he discovers that someone
else believes in him and is willing to trust him.

RALPH WALDO EMERSON

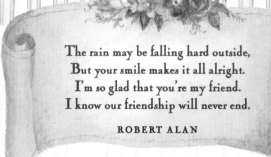

The rain may be falling hard outside,
But your smile makes it all alright.
I'm so glad that you're my friend.
I know our friendship will never end.

ROBERT ALAN

We cannot tell the precise moment when friendship is formed. As in filling a vessel drop by drop, there is at last a drop which makes it run over. So in a series of kindness there is, at last, one which makes the heart run over.

JAMES BOSWELL

A real friend is one who walks in when the rest of the world walks out.

WALTER WINCHELL

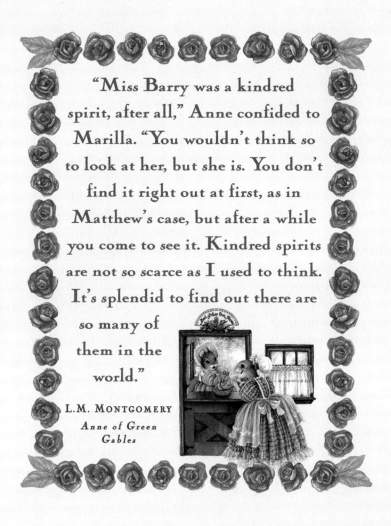

"Miss Barry was a kindred spirit, after all," Anne confided to Marilla. "You wouldn't think so to look at her, but she is. You don't find it right out at first, as in Matthew's case, but after a while you come to see it. Kindred spirits are not so scarce as I used to think. It's splendid to find out there are so many of them in the world."

L.M. MONTGOMERY
Anne of Green Gables

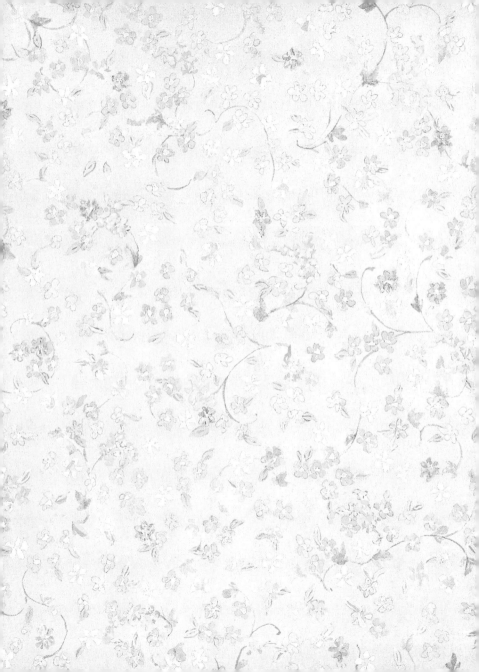

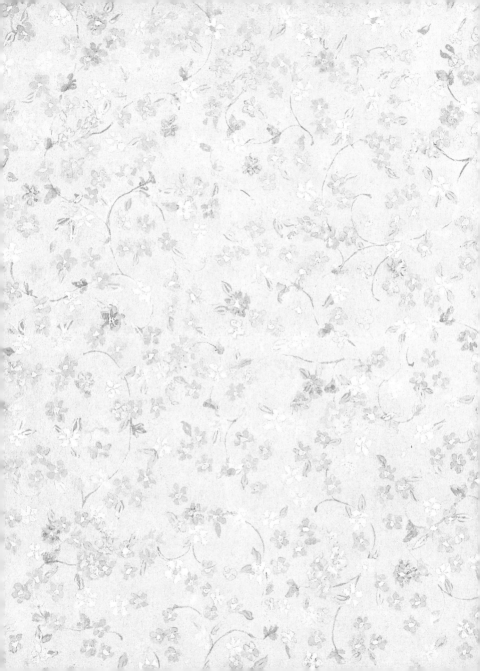